THE
HEART
OF
PETER
MARSHALL'S
FAITH

THE
HEART
OF
PETER
MARSHALL'S
FAITH

Two Inspirational Messages by

PETER MARSHALL

from Mr. Jones, Meet the Master

. . . .

FLEMING H. REVELL COMPANY

Printed in the United States of America

LIBRARY OF CONGRESS CATALOG CARD NUMBER: 56–5237

Westwood, N. J. — 316 Third Avenue
London E. C. 4 — 29 Ludgate Hill
Glasgow C. 2 — 229 Bothwell Street

In these two sermons is the heart of Peter Marshall's faith and preaching—the gist of what he believed about some of life's most important relationships in this world, and fulfillment in the next.

CATHERINE MARSHALL

CONTENTS

DR. MARSHALL wrote "The Grave In the Garden"—one of his most eloquent sermons—in an hour of inspiration following the reading of Beverley Nichols' book, *The Fool Hath Said* (Doubleday Doran & Company, Inc.).

Prayer

*God of our fathers and our God, give us
the faith to believe in the ultimate triumph
of righteousness. . . . We pray for the bi-
focals of faith that see the despair and the
need of the hour but also see, further on,
the patience of our God working out His
plan in the world He has made. . . .
Through Jesus our Lord.* AMEN.

The Resurrection never becomes a fact of experience until the risen Christ lives in the heart of the believer.

From I HAVE THE KEYS

The Grave in the Garden

IT IS AN OLD QUESTION—as old as death itself—and as new . . .

We find it in the oldest part of the Old Book, the fourteenth verse of the fourteenth chapter of Job:

"If a man die, shall he live again?"

It is a question that is found in every sob in times of bereavement.

It is a question that knocks with gloved hand on the door of the weeping heart.

But how strange to say "if"—"if a man die!"
There is no "if." All of us must die.

A more exact interpretation of the question asked in Job would be to say, "When a man dies, after a man dies, will he live again?"

That is the question!

Is life possible after death?

Millions of people glibly repeat the Apostles' Creed: "I believe in the resurrection of the body."

We speak of resurrection, but have we seen it?
We try to disguise death with flowers—

> flowers on the casket
> wreaths on the doorknob
> flowers heaped on the cold grave.

We embalm the body to make it look lifelike.
We color the cheeks and tint the pallid face, as though to deceive ourselves.

We even dress the body in the departed tenant's best clothes, but after we are finished, it is still a dead body, without any life.

The facts concerning Jesus of Nazareth are, according to the Church, that He lived

> He died

> and He arose from the dead.

Can the Church justify such a contention?

He lived, as no intelligent student can deny.
He died. That fact nobody need deny.
He died quivering on the cross, after about six hours of agony and suffering.
To make sure of His death, one of the soldiers pierced His side with a spear, and the last remaining drops of His blood were poured out to prove that His love was stronger than death.

The soldiers who had carried out the detail of the hammer and the nails were quite satisfied that He was dead.

"That one didn't take long," they said, as they prepared to fall in line and march back to their barracks.

They did not even take the trouble to break His legs, for it was plain to be seen that He was finished.

It is reflected in the hopelessness of His disciples. As the afternoon sun threw the lengthening shadows of the three crosses down the hillside, and the bronze armor of the soldiers reflected its light, a brooding sadness descended upon His disciples, who looked at each other in a puzzled grief that knew no speech.

Three years before, the Master had called them to become fishers of men. Now that His flame had died away they would once more become fishers of fish.
Such was their mood.

Their King crucified like a criminal.
Their Messiah ending up—not on a throne, but on a cross,
hailed as King on Sunday, and dead like a common thief on Friday.

They remained the despairing survivors of a broken cause as they stumbled blindly down the hill, their eyes filled with tears they could not stop.

They were the very picture of men without any hope
    utterly crushed . . . beaten . . .
        disappointed . . .
In their faces there was the stark, dreadful look of hopeless despair.

"I go a fishing," said Peter. What else was there left to do?
Back to the old familiar boats with their worn seats
    their patched sails
  and their high rudders,

back to the mending of their nets,
sadder but wiser men, finding the road back a hard road to take.

Jesus was a dead man now, very much like any other dead man. So when even the Roman authorities were satisfied that they had seen the last of this strange, troublesome Dreamer, His enemies went to Pilate asking him to set a watch of soldiers about the tomb for three days.

Remembering that He had said He would rise again, and being afraid that His disciples would come and steal the body away, they insisted on sealing with their own official seal the huge stone that blocked the entrance to the grave.
Pilate granted their request saying:
"Ye have a watch, go your way, make it as sure as you can."
We are not told whether Pilate smiled a sardonic smile as he spoke, but Matthew adds the most ironic sentence in literature:
"So they went and made the sepulchre sure, sealing the stone and setting a watch."

Thus they took every precaution against fraud.

A broken seal would reveal that the grave had been opened, but soldiers would be on guard to prevent that happening.

And as they made their way down the hill and back to the city, such thoughts as these ran through their minds:

"He is finished.
We shall hear no more of Him.
Now His fishermen can get back to their nets and their boats . . .
We shall hear no more talk about His kingdom.
As for this Jesus, He is dead enough.
There is no doubt about that.

"Even though He had a breath of life left in the bloodless body, it is now being suffocated by the hundredweight of spice with which He was embalmed.

"He, who said He could summon twelve legions of angels to His assistance, died crying that He was forsaken.
He will trouble us no more."

Thus they left Him on Friday evening—just before the Sabbath began, His dead body hastily embalmed,
wrapped in bandages on which a hundred pounds of myrrh had been hastily spread . . .
the tomb closed with a huge stone and soldiers standing guard around it.

Then came Sunday morning.

The first rays of the early morning sun cast a great light that caused the dew drops on the flowers to sparkle like diamonds.
The atmosphere of the garden was changed . . .

It was the same garden . . . yet strangely different.
The heaviness of despair was gone.
and there was a new note in the singing of the birds.

Suddenly, at a certain hour between sunset and dawn, in that new tomb which had belonged to Joseph of Arimathea, there was a strange stirring, a fluttering of unseen forces . . .
a whirring of angel wings
the rustle as of the breath of God moving through the garden.

Strong, immeasurable forces poured life back into the dead body they had laid upon the cold stone slab;
and the dead man rose up

came out of the grave clothes
walked to the threshold of the tomb,
stood swaying for a moment on His wounded feet,
and walked out into the moonlit garden.

We can almost hear in our hearts the faint sigh as the life spirit fluttered back into the tortured body, and smell in our own nostrils the medley of strange scents that floated back to Him
of linen and bandages . . .
     and spices
          and close air and blood. .

Then came a group of women as soon as they could, bringing spices and materials with which to complete the hasty anointing of their Lord.

They came with all the materials with which to anoint a dead body,
and when they came to the grave in the garden, they found that the stone had been rolled away from the door of it, and the grave was empty.

Here is John's account of what followed:

"But Mary stood without at the sepulchre weeping: and as she wept, she stooped down, and looked into the sepulchre, And seeth two angels in white sitting, the one at the head, and the other at the feet, where the body of Jesus had lain.
And they say unto her, Woman, why weepest thou? She saith unto them, Because they have taken away my Lord, and I know not where they have laid him.

"And when she had thus said, she turned herself back, and saw Jesus standing, and knew not that it was Jesus.

Jesus saith unto her, Woman, why weepest thou? whom seekest thou? She, supposing him to be the gardener, saith unto him, Sir, if thou have borne him hence, tell me where thou hast laid him, and I will take him away.
Jesus saith unto her, Mary. She turned herself, and saith unto him, Rabboni; which is to say, Master."

There were two names spoken, "Mary" and "Rabboni."
She heard her own name spoken as only one Voice could speak it—gently echoing in the garden.
And there was her "Rabboni"—the breathless "Master!" as she saw His face.

Christ had spoken her name, and all of heaven was in it.
She uttered only one word, and all of earth was in it.

If we believe this, it is one of the loveliest stories in literature.
It is a story over which, without shame, men might weep.
It is a story which we cannot read without feeling a lump in our throats.

If we do not believe it, it is a clever and shameful lie!
Does it sound like a lie to you?
Does it have a hollow ring of uncertainty or falsehood,
Do you not rather get the feel of truth in it?

"Jesus saith unto her, Mary . . .
She turned herself and saith unto him, Rabboni, which is to say, Master."

Is it all a trick? Are we all deluded fools?
No, we are not deluded—
No fact in history is better established,
    more scientifically established, than this one.

The disciples did not expect this to happen!
Their belief in the Resurrection was not some fantastic idea that
had been wafted in from the swamps of their fevered imagina-
tions.

It was not some romantic wish out of their dream-house, not
the result of wishful thinking,
    for it came as a complete shock
        unexpected
            bewildering.

When Mary Magdalene and Joanna and Mary, the mother of
James, and other women came breathlessly from the empty
tomb, shaking with an extraordinary excitement and blurting
out the news to the disciples, we are told:
    "and their words seemed to them as idle tales, and they be-
    lieved them not."

Over and over again this point is emphasized.
Read the stories for yourselves!

Read Luke, or the story of Thomas, the dogged unbeliever, as
John tells it,
    "except I shall see in his hands the print of the nails, and put
    my finger into the print of the nails, and thrust my hand into
    his side, *I will not believe.*"

That was no wishful thinking, was it?

Eight days passed by. The disciples were gathered together. This
time Thomas was there. Suddenly Jesus was with them in the
room, and He said to Thomas.
    "Reach hither thy finger, and behold my hands; and reach

20

hither thy hand, and thrust it into my side: and be not faith-less, but believing."

And Thomas answered and said unto Him, "My Lord and my God."

Now, if one man says he has seen a dead person alive, you may believe him or not, according to your opinion of his trustworthiness.

If ten men tell you that they have, at the same time, seen this dead person alive, talking
walking in newness of life,
you begin to be impressed.

If five hundred men tell you that they have seen Someone who was dead . . .
well, you must admit that you are in a startling minority.

If you deny the reality of the Resurrection appearances, you are in precisely that minority.

The Resurrection of Christ was regarded by the disciples as something which is as indisputable historically as the death of President Wilson.

It did not occur to them, as they spoke or as they wrote, to argue about it, any more than it would occur to a Senator making a speech in the Senate to say:

"Since the death of President Wilson,
that is to say, if he is really dead,
and if his body is not mysteriously spirited away; if he is not at this moment living in a shack in South Georgia with a heavy growth of whiskers. . . ."

They were writing down on papyrus stupendous things . . . within hailing distance of the events themselves.
The winds had hardly had time to cover up His footprints in the sands of Judea.

As Beverley Nichols puts it:

"The rain had hardly had time to wash away, with its callous tears the blood from the rotting wood of a deserted Cross."

Do you think their story is an invention?
Could *you* invent that sort of story?

And would you invent it so that you might be crucified upside down, like Peter?
 Or have your head chopped off, like Paul, outside the city of Rome,
  or be stoned to death—like Stephen?

Why would they persist in a lie, if every time they insisted it was true, they were driving nails into their own coffins?

John and Peter, as they went into the grave that morning, did not know what to think, until they saw what was inside the grave —and then they believed.

The inside of the tomb revealed something that proved the Resurrection. What was it?
Let us turn to the narrative again and read carefully:

"Then cometh Simon Peter following him, and went into the sepulchre, and seeth the linen clothes lie,
And the napkin, that was about his head, not lying with the linen clothes, but wrapped together in a place by itself.

Then went in also that other disciple, which came first to the sepulchre, and he saw, and believed" (JOHN 20:6–8).

In this connection, it is well for us to remember that the stone was rolled away from the door, not to permit Christ to come out, but to enable the disciples to go in.

Notice what it was they saw.
They saw the linen clothes lying, not unwound and carefully folded, as some people appear to think—
    not thrown aside as is a covering when one rises from bed,
but lying there on the stone slab *in the shape of the body.*

True, the napkin had been removed and folded, but the grave clothes were lying there mute, but eloquent evidence that a living organism had come out.

The grave clothes lay like the shriveled, cracked shell of a cocoon left behind when the moth has emerged and hoisted her bright sails in the sunshine . . .
or, more accurately, like a glove from which the hand has been removed, the fingers of which still retain the shape of the hand.

In that manner, the grave clothes were lying, collapsed a little —slightly deflated—because there was between the rolls of bandages a considerable weight of spices, but there lay the linen cloth that had been wound round the body of Christ.

It was when they saw *that,* that the disciples believed.

The Greek word here for "see" is *not* to behold as one looks at a spectacle, not to see as the watchmaker who peers through his magnifying glass.
It means to see with inner sight that leads one to a conclusion.

23

It is perception
  reflection
    understanding—more than sight.
  Do you *see?*

It is to see, as one who reasons from the effect to the cause, and
when John and Peter reasoned from what they saw in the tomb,
they arrived at the conclusion
        the unshakable
      unassailable
    certain conviction
that Jesus Christ had risen from the dead.

Then, what happened?
Suddenly Peter is facing the foes of Jesus with a reckless courage.
He speaks boldly:
    "Ye men of Israel, hear these words; Jesus of Nazareth, a
    man approved of God among you by miracles and wonders
    and signs, which God did by him in the midst of you, as ye
    yourselves also know:
    him, being delivered by the determinate counsel and fore-
    knowledge of God, ye have taken, and by wicked hands have
    crucified and slain:
    whom God hath raised up, having loosed the pains of death:
    because it was not possible that he should be holden of it."
    (ACTS 2:22–24).

because it was not possible that he should be holden of it
not the same man. He is different—
    very, very different.

24

What had happened?

The undeniable fact is this: the disciples of Jesus were scattered
  downcast
    hopeless
      with a sense of tragic loss
and then, in a few days, they were thrilling with victory, completely changed.

As Dr. Buttrick has said,
"Why did these men suddenly rise from their bemoanings, and
with light on their faces, fairly spring on the world with the
message of a living Saviour, for whom they were willing to suffer
any persecution?"

There is no "In Memoriam" note in the narratives.
After the death of Christ, every page is filled with the sense of
the "abiding and empowering presence of Christ."

They were all thrilled beyond fear in the stupendous knowledge
that Christ was *alive,*
and they went about rejoicing in a joy behind pain.
Why?

"Ah, just a delusion," suggests the man who is frankly skeptical
of the whole business.
"Miracles! They don't happen. They just simply don't happen!
Don't make it any more difficult for me to believe, then, by giv-
ing me another problem.

"All this story of a dead body becoming alive again and coming
out of grave-clothes and bandages,
and walking out into a garden and out of sight.

These tales of mysterious appearances of a body going
    through a door
   appearing and disappearing
  eating solid food and yet vanishing like a mirage . . .
All this talk of ignorant fishermen seeing angels sitting on a rock.
Don't ask me to believe all that. It is too much," says the skeptic.

Very well. You are sitting in your own living room.
By your side is a radio.
You reach out a hand and turn on a switch. In a few seconds,
the room is filled with music.

A woman's voice is singing "I know that my Redeemer liveth."
But you are not in the mood for that sort of thing.
And, besides, you don't like her voice, and you reach out a bored
hand and turn it off again.
Silence.

Silence? Why, the music is still going on. She is still singing. Oh,
no, she isn't. We turned off the radio!

Well, what has that got to do with it?

Simply this. That when you turn off the radio, you don't turn
off the music. And whether we believe it or not,
   Schubert is still in the room,
     (by courtesy of somebody's hair tonic),
   and Mendelssohn
     (through the kindness of somebody else's baked spaghetti)
   and Beethoven and all the music of the earth.

There are voices pleading
   voices praying

and voices that whisper
     and voices that are sad.

They are all around us and we sit there—wrapped in silence.

And out of it all one Voice speaks. We may stick our fingers in our ears.

We may shut our eyes,
and still we can hear the Voice: "Lo, I am with you always, even unto the end of the world."

And we say to ourselves, "It is all madness—
     beautiful madness
          superstition
               lovely, sweet superstition,
but it is not true. It cannot be so . . ."

And then the Voice again, "Be still, and know that I am God."

Is it true?
Is Christ really risen from the dead?

As that question begins to knock—gently—on your heart's door, you realize that you have gone back through the centuries to when the world was nineteen hundred years younger,
back to the country of the camel,
     and sandaled footprints in the sands of Palestine . . .
back to the time of the Roman eagle fluttering over bronze breastplates
     shining in the Syrian sun
back to the days of the Cæsars.

And you feel quite funny—almost ridiculous—for you have your miscroscope in your hand
     your measuring tape

> your litmus paper
> > your biology textbook
> > > your test tube
> > > > and your college diploma.

In the half-shadow in the womb of time your microscope glitters like a diamond.
Your tape measure gleams like a line of gold.
Your litmus paper is a purple ribbon from a royal standard.
Your test tube, a silver bugle to sound a note of triumph,
And the noise and confusion of unbelief has died away.

And in the quiet Easter morning you are standing in front of a grave in a garden, and you see a stone in the doorway, but the stone is moving . . . is moving.*

And before you are aware of it, you will realize suddenly that Someone is standing beside you, and your eyes are fixed on His hand, and you see a mark in the palm of it, like the print of a nail.

And as a great realization dawns over you, you hear His voice:
"Lo, I am with you always, even unto the end of the world."
"Whosoever believeth in me, though he were dead, yet shall he live,
and whosoever liveth and believeth in me, shall never die . . ."
"Because I live, ye shall live also."

Because we can't stand it any longer—in the secret places of our hearts, we cry out to God for help—and then it comes, the supreme miracle for which we have been seeking.

It is so tremendous a thing that we can't describe it.

* Dr. Marshall is indebted here to Beverley Nichols for the illustrations of the microscope, measuring tape, litmus paper, etc.

It is so delicate a thing that we can't even bring it into view for anybody else to look at.

We can never explain it to anybody else.
We know only that it is true.

The Voice has said: "Because I live, ye shall live also."

Our hearts knew all along it must be so.
It was what we wanted to hear, and now that we have heard it, we feel that we have solved the mystery of life.

"If a man die, shall he live again?"
Yes, because the Resurrection is a fact.
Aye, and I, too, shall live, because I know it's true.

Prayer

Our Father, we are beginning to understand at last that the things that are wrong with our world are the sum total of all the things that are wrong with us as individuals. Thou hast made us after Thine image, and our hearts can find no rest until they rest in Thee.

We are too Christian really to enjoy sinning and too fond of sinning really to enjoy Christianity. Most of us know perfectly well what we ought to do; our trouble is that we do not want to do it. Thy help is our only hope. Make us want to do what is right, and give us the ability to do it.

In the name of Christ our Lord. AMEN.

There is beauty in homely things which
many people have never seen. For instance,
do you know
Sunlight through a jar of beach-plum jelly;
  A rainbow in soapsuds in dishwater;
An egg yolk in a blue bowl;
  White ruffled curtains sifting moonlight;
The color of cranberry glass;
  A little cottage with blue shutters;
Crimson roses in an old stone crock;
  The smell of newly baked bread;
Candlelight on old brass;
  The soft brown of a cocker's eyes?

From LETTER TO A MOTHER

Keepers of the Springs

O NCE UPON A TIME, a certain town grew up at the foot of a
mountain range. It was sheltered in the lee of the protect-
ing heights, so that the wind that shuddered at the doors and
flung handfuls of sleet against the window panes was a wind
whose fury was spent.

High up in the hills, a strange and quiet forest dweller took it
upon himself to be the Keeper of the Springs.

He patrolled the hills and wherever he found a spring, he cleaned
its brown pool of silt and fallen leaves, of mud and mould
and took way from the spring all foreign matter, so that the
water which bubbled up through the sand ran down clean and
cold and pure.

It leaped sparkling over rocks and dropped joyously in crystal cascades until, swollen by other streams, it became a river of life to the busy town.

Millwheels were whirled by its rush.
Gardens were refreshed by its waters.
Fountains threw it like diamonds into the air.
Swans sailed on its limpid surface
and children laughed as they played on its banks in the sunshine.

But the City Council was a group of hard-headed, hard-boiled business men. They scanned the civic budget and found in it the salary of a Keeper of the Springs.

Said the Keeper of the Purse: "Why should we pay this romance ranger? We never see him; he is not necessary to our town's work life. If we build a reservoir just above the town, we can dispense with his services and save his salary."

Therefore, the City Council voted to dispense with the unnecessary cost of a Keeper of the Springs, and to build a cement reservoir.

So the Keeper of the Springs no longer visited the brown pools but watched from the heights while they built the reservoir.

When it was finished, it soon filled up with water. to be sure, but the water did not seem to be the same.
It did not seem to be as clean, and a green scum soon befouled its stagnant surface.

There were constant troubles with the delicate machinery of the mills, for it was often clogged with slime, and the swans found another home above the town.

At last, an epidemic raged, and the clammy, yellow fingers of sickness reached into every home in every street and lane.

The City Council met again. Sorrowfully, it faced the city's plight, and frankly it acknowledged the mistake of the dismissal of the Keeper of the Springs.

They sought him out in his hermit hut high in the hills, and begged him to return to his former joyous labor.
Gladly he agreed, and began once more to make his rounds.

It was not long until pure water came lilting down under tunnels of ferns and mosses and to sparkle in the cleansed reservoir.

Millwheels turned again as of old.

 Stenches disappeared.

  Sickness waned

and convalescent children playing in the sun laughed again because the swans had come back.

Do not think me fanciful

 too imaginative

  or too extravagant in my language

when I say that I think of women, and particularly of our mothers, as Keepers of the Springs. The phrase, while poetic, is true and descriptive.

We feel its warmth . . .

 its softening influence . . .

and however forgetful we have been . . .

 however much we have taken for granted life's precious gifts we are conscious of wistful memories that surge out of the past—

 the sweet

  tender

   poignant fragrances of love.

Nothing that has been said
  nothing that could be said
    or that ever will be said,
would be eloquent enough, expressive enough, or adequate to
make articulate that peculiar emotion we feel to our mothers.

So I shall make my tribute a plea for Keepers of the Springs,
who will be faithful to their tasks.

There never has been a time when there was a greater need for
Keepers of the Springs,
or when there were more polluted springs to be cleansed.
If the home fails, the country is doomed. The breakdown of
home life and influence will mark the breakdown of the nation.

If the Keepers of the Springs desert their posts or are unfaithful
to their responsibilities the future outlook of this country is black
indeed.

This generation needs Keepers of the Springs who will be cou-
rageous enough to cleanse the springs that have been polluted.

It is not an easy task—nor is it a popular one, but it must be
done for the sake of the children, and the young women of today
must do it.

The emancipation of womanhood began with Christianity, and
it ends with Christianity.
It had its beginning one night nineteen hundred years ago when
there came to a woman named Mary a vision and a message
from Heaven.

She saw the rifted clouds of glory
  and the hidden battlements of heaven.

She heard an angelic annunciation of the almost incredible news that she of all the women on earth . . .

of all the Marys in history . . .

was to be the only one who should ever wear entwined the red rose of maternity and the white rose of virginity.

It was told her—and all Keepers of the Springs know how such messages come—that she should be the mother of the Saviour of the world.

It was nineteen hundred years ago "when Jesus Himself a baby deigned to be and bathed in baby tears His deity" . . . and on that night, when that tiny Child lay in the straw of Bethlehem, began the emancipation of womanhood.

When He grew up and began to teach the way of life, He ushered woman into a new place in human relations. He accorded her a new dignity and crowned her with a new glory, so that wherever the Christian evangel has gone for nineteen centuries, the daughters of Mary have been

respected

revered

remembered

and loved,

for men have recognized that womanhood is a sacred and a noble thing, that women are of finer clay . . .

are more in touch with the angels of God and have the noblest function that life affords.

Wherever Christianity has spread, for nineteen hundred years men have bowed and adored.

It remained for the twentieth century,

in the name of progress

in the name of tolerance
in the name of broadmindedness
in the name of freedom
to pull her down from her throne and try to make her like a
man.

She wanted equality. For nineteen hundred years she had not
been equal—she had been superior.
But now, they said, she wanted equality, and in order to obtain
it, she had to step down.

And so it is, that in the name of broadminded tolerance a man's
vices have now become a woman's.
Twentieth century tolerance has won for woman
the right to become intoxicated
the right to have an alcoholic breath
the right to smoke
to work like a man
to act like a man—
for is she not man's equal?

Today they call it "progress" . . .
but tomorrow—oh, you Keepers of the Springs, they must be
made to see that it is not progress.

No nation has ever made any progress in a downward direction.
No people ever became great by lowering their standards.
No people ever became good by adopting a looser morality.

It is not progress when the moral tone is lower than it was.
It is not progress when purity is not as sweet.
It is not progress when womanhood has lost its fragrance.
Whatever else it is, it is not progress!

We need Keepers of the Springs who will realize that what is socially correct may not be morally right.

Our country needs today women who will lead us back to an old-fashioned morality
   to old-fashioned decency
      to old-fashioned purity and sweetness
for the sake of the next generation, if for no other reason.

This generation has seen an entirely new type of womanhood emerge from the bewildering confusion of our time.
We have in the United States today a higher standard of living than in any other country, or at any other time in the world's history.

We have more automobiles, more picture shows,
   more telephones, more money
      more swing bands, more radios,
         more television sets, more night clubs,
         more crime, and more divorce
than any other nation in the world.

Modern mothers want their children to enjoy the advantages of this new day.
They want them, if possible, to have a college diploma to hang on their bedroom wall,
and what many of them regard as equally important—a bid to a fraternity or a sorority.

They are desperately anxious that their daughters will be popular, although the price of this popularity may not be considered until it is too late.

In short, they want their children to succeed, but the usual definition of success, in keeping with the trend of our day, is largely materialistic.

The result of all this is that the modern child brought up in a decent.
  cultured
    comfortable
      but thoroughly irreligious home.

All around us, living in the very shadow of our large churches and beautiful cathedrals, children are growing up without a particle of religious training or influence.

The parents of such children have usually completely given up the search for religious moorings.
At first, they probably had some sort of vague idealism as to what their children should be taught.

They recall something of the religious instruction received when they were children, and they feel that something like that ought to be passed on to the children of today, but they can't do it,
  because the simple truth is that they have nothing to give.
Our modern broadmindedness has taken religious education out of the day schools.
Our modern way of living and our modern irreligion have taken it out of the homes.

There remains only one place where it may be obtained,
  and that is in the Sunday School,
but it is no longer fashionable to attend Sunday School.

The result is that there is very little religious education, and parents who lack it themselves are not able to give it to their children—so it is a case of "the blind leading the blind," and both children and parents will almost invariably end up in the ditch of uncertainty and irreligion.

As you think of your own mother, remembering her with love and gratitude—in wishful yearning
   or lonely longing . . .
I am quite sure that the memories that warm and soften your heart are not at all like the memories the children of today will have . . .

For you are, no doubt, remembering the smell of the starch in your mother's apron
   or the smell of a newly ironed blouse
     the smell of newly baked bread
       the fragrance of the violets she had pinned on her breast.

It would be such a pity if all that one could remember would be the aroma of toasted tobacco
   or nicotine
  and the offensive odor of beer on the breath!

The challenge to twentieth-century motherhood is as old as motherhood itself.
Although the average American mother has advantages that pioneer women never knew—material advantages
    education
    culture
   advances made by science and medicine
although the modern mother knows a great deal more about sterilization, diets, health, calories, germs, drugs, medicines, and

vitamins, than her mother did, there is one subject about which she does not know as much—

and that is God.

The modern challenge to motherhood is the eternal challenge—that of being godly women.

The very phrase sounds strange in our ears. We never hear it now.

We hear about every other kind of women—
   beautiful women,
     smart women,
       sophisticated women,
         career women,
           talented women,
             divorced women,
but so seldom do we hear of a godly woman—or of a godly man either, for that matter.

I believe women come nearer fulfilling their God-given function in the home than anywhere else.

It is a much nobler thing to be a good wife than to be Miss America.

It is a greater achievement to establish a Christian home than it is to produce a second-rate novel filled with filth.

It is a far, far better thing in the realm of morals to be old-fashioned than to be ultramodern.

The world has enough women who know how to hold their cocktails
   who have lost all their illusions
     and their faith.

The world has enough women who know how to be smart.
It needs women who are willing to be simple.
The world has enough women who know how to be brilliant.
It needs some who will be brave.
The world has enough women who are popular.
It needs more who are pure.
We need women, and men too, who would rather be morally right than socially correct.

Let us not fool ourselves—without Christianity
without Christian education
without the principles of Christ
inculcated into young life, we are simply rearing pagans.

Physically, they will be perfect.
Intellectually, they will be brilliant.
But spiritually, they will be pagan.
Let us not fool ourselves.

The school is making no attempt to teach the principles of Christ.
The Church alone cannot do it.
They can never be taught to a child unless the mother herself knows them and practices them every day.

If you have no prayer life yourself it is rather a useless gesture to make your child say his prayers every night.

If you never enter a church it is rather futile to send your child to Sunday School.

If you make a practice of telling social lies it will be difficult to teach your child to be truthful.

If you say cutting things about your neighbors and about fellow members in the church it will be hard for your child to learn the meaning of kindness.

The twentieth-century challenge to motherhood—when it is all boiled down—is that mothers will have an experience of God . . . a reality which they can pass on to their children. For the newest of the sciences is beginning to realize, after a study of the teachings of Christ from the standpoint of psychology, that only as human beings discover and follow these inexorably spiritual laws will they find the happiness and contentment which we all seek.

A minister tells of going to a hospital to visit a mother whose first child had been born.
She was distinctly a modern girl.
Her home was about average for young married people.

"When I came into the room she was propped up in bed writing.
'Come in,' she said, smiling. 'I'm in the midst of house-cleaning and I want your help.'

"I had never heard of a woman house-cleaning while in a hospital bed. Her smile was contagious—she seemed to have found a new and jolly idea.

" 'I've had a wonderful chance to think here,' she began, 'and it may help me to get things straightened out in my mind if I can talk to you.'
She put down her pencil and pad, and folded her hands. Then she took a long breath and started:

" 'Ever since I was a little girl, I hated any sort of restraint. I always wanted to be free. When I finished high school, I took a business course and got a job—not because I needed the money —but because I wanted to be on my own.

" 'Before Joe and I were married, we used to say that we would not be slaves to each other. And after we married our apartment became headquarters for a crowd just like us. We weren't really bad—but we did just what we pleased.'

"She stopped for a minute and smiled ruefully.
'God didn't mean much to us—we ignored Him. None of us wanted children—or we thought we didn't. And when I knew I was going to have a baby I was afraid.'

"She stopped again and looked puzzled. 'Isn't it funny, the things you used to think?'
She had almost forgotten I was there—she was speaking to the old girl she had been before her great adventure.

"Then remembering me suddenly—she went on: 'Where was I? Oh, yes, well, things are different now. I'm not free any more and I don't want to be. And the first thing I must do is to clean house.'

"Here she picked up the sheet of paper lying on the counter-pane. 'That's my house-cleaning list. You see, when I take Betty home from the hospital with me—our apartment will be her home—not just mine and Joe's.

" 'And it isn't fit for her now. Certain things will have to go— for Betty's sake. And I've got to house-clean my heart and mind. I'm not just myself—I'm Betty's mother.
And that means I need God. I can't do my job without Him.
Won't you pray for Betty and me and Joe,
    and for our new home?'

"And I saw in her all the mothers of today—mothers in tiny apartments and on lonely farms . . .

Mothers in great houses and in suburban cottages who are meeting the age-old challenge—'that of bringing their children to the love and knowledge of God.'

"And I seemed to see our Saviour—with His arms full of children of far-away Judea—saying to that mother and to all mothers—the old invitation so much needed in these times:
'Suffer the little children to come
unto me and forbid them not, for of
such is the kingdom of God.' "

I believe that this generation of young people has courage enough to face the challenging future.

I believe that their idealism is not dead. I believe that they have the same bravery and the same devotion to the things worth while that their grandmothers had.

I have every confidence that they are anxious to preserve the best of our heritage, and God knows if we lose it here in this country it is forever gone.

I believe that the women of today will not be unmindful of their responsibilities; that is why I have dared to speak so honestly.
Keepers of the Springs, we salute you!